The Solace of Wild Places

The Solace of Wild Places

Kathryn Jones

ISBN:978-1-962148-21-4
LOC: 2025945377
Editor: Rylee Wenzel

Lamar University Literary Press
Beaumont, TX

For Dan, for my family, and the large family of friends who yearn for places of wild wonder.

Recent Poetry from Lamar University Literary Press

Lisa Adams, *Xuai*
Walter Bargen, *Radiation Diary: Return to the Sea*
Christine Boldt, *In Every Tatter*
Devan Burton, *A Room for Us*
Jerry Bradley, *Collapsing into Possibility*
Mark Busby, *Through Our Times*
Julie Chappell, *Mad Habits of a Life*
Stan Crawford, *Resisting Gravity*
Glover Davis, *Academy of Dreams*
Wendy Dunmeyer, *My Grandmother's Last Letter*
Chris Ellery, *Elder Tree*
Kelly Ann Ellis, *The Hungry Ghost Diner*
Dede Fox, *On Wings of Silence*
Alan Gann, *That's Entertainment*
Larry Griffin, *Cedar Plums*
Lynn Hoggard, *First Light*
Michael Jennings, *Crossings: A Record of Travel*
Markham Johnson, *Dear Dreamland*
Betsy Joseph & Chip Dameron, *Relatively Speaking*
Jim McGarrah, *A Balancing Act*
J. Pittman McGehee, *Nod of Knowing*
David Meischen, *Caliche Road Poems*
Laurence Musgrove, *A Stranger's Heart*
Benjamin Myers, *The Family Book of Martyrs*
Janice Northerns, *Some Electric Hum*
Godspower Oboido, *Wandering Feet on Pebbled Shores*
Dave Oliphant, *Summing Up: Selected Poems*
Nathanael O'Reilly, *Landmarks*
Carol Coffee Reposa, *Sailing West*
Jan Seale, *Particulars*
Steven Schroeder, *the moon, not the finger, pointing*
C.W. Smith, *The Museum of Marriage*
Vincent Spina, *The Sumptuous Hills of Gulfport*
W.K. Stratton, *Betrayal Creek*
Ken Waldman, *Sports Page*
Loretta Diane Walker, *Ode to My Mother's Voice*
Dan Williams, *At the Gates, a Refuge of Milkweed and Sunflowers*
Jonas Zdanys, *The Angled Road*

For information on these and other Lamar University Literary
Press books go to www.Lamar.edu/literarypress

Acknowledgments

Many thanks to the editors of the following journals and anthologies for publishing some of the poems (or earlier versions of them) in this book.

Langdon Review of the Arts in Texas, Vol. 17, 2020-2021, and Vol. 19, 2022-2023
Last Stanza Poetry Journal, issues #14 and #15 (Stackfeed Press, 2023 and 2024)
Lone Star Poetry (Kallisto Gaia Press, 2022)
Odes and Elegies: Eco-Poetry from the Texas Gulf Coast (Lamar University Literary Press, 2021)
An Orchid's Guide to Life (chapbook, Finishing Line Press, 2024)
TexasPoetryAssignment.org
Unknotting the Line: The Poetry in Prose (Dos Gatos Press, 2023)

*Wilderness is not only a condition of nature,
but a state of mind and mood and heart.* – Ansel Adams

CONTENTS

III.   Places of Shelter

Introduction

Some places never leave us when we physically leave. The places that stay with me are close to nature—the Texas Gulf Coast where I grew up; the canyons, deserts, and big sky of Far West Texas and northern New Mexico, where I feel most spiritually at home; and my current physical home on a piece of land eight miles south of Glen Rose at the top of the Texas Hill Country. They shaped my identity—they are all "where I come from."

After living in cities throughout my life, in 2005 I moved to a rural area in Bosque County just beyond a string of hills called the Seven Knobs. To the west, land rises and falls in waves of limestone ridges and cedar. Blue mesas—Chalk Mountain to the north and Flat Top Mountain to the south—notch the horizon. I know this patch of land and it knows me.

These wild places constantly remake themselves with the seasons, the weather and climate, even the time of day. As you get to know the plants, the animals, the rocks, and the ever-changing rhythms of place, you change, too.

The poems in this volume explore my relationship with place. Because of the strong connection with pieces of land and bodies of water, I have become the person I was always meant to be. It is a sixth sense that many of us share—the sense of place.

–*Kathryn Jones*

I.

Places by Water

Hiraeth

My ancestors came from Wales;
I have never been there, but share
their constant longing

for something I cannot describe
but know in my bones—
hiraeth, a Welsh word for

an incompleteness that yearns,
like a soul wandering alone in green hills
looking for its mate,

peering into the cave of melancholy,
finding nothing there but darkness,
pressing onward to search

for tender light in a place that feels
like home but more—
the place where my spirit dwells.

Bird's Eye View

I hear faint cries high in the sky
on the first chilly day of fall
and long to fly away and join them,
hitchhike on beating wings,
align with sandhill cranes in flight,
sun and wind on my back,
head by instinct to a place I know—
but when I get there, it's changed
and I change it again with my presence,
then return in early spring to find
the refuge I sought was here,
in this place, all along.

Shell Hunting

Padre Island in summer,
white foam ruffles on green water,
pink ruffles on my swimsuit and bonnet,
smells of seaweed and suntan lotion.
My mother held my tiny hand. *Jump!*
she said as she lifted me above the waves.

She gave me a plastic bucket and shovel
for scooping shells we found. Later
she taught me the names: Angel Wing,
Shark's Eye, Calico Scallop, Sundial,
and her favorite, Lightning Whelk,
pearly pink mouth open to secret chambers.

Hold it to your ear, my mother said.
You can hear the sea.

Years later, the memory pulls at me
like the moon pulls tides. She is not there
to lift me over the waves now. I remember
the names of all the shells that fill
the clear glass vase on my desk. The whelk
rests on top like a crown.

I hold it to my ear every day so I can hear
my mother's voice floating on the sea.

Beach Glass

Among the flotsam and pebbles,
a jewel on the sand offered up by the Gulf,
begat in brokenness—a bottle tossed,
a jar shattered, a candy dish fallen off a boat,
a crystal vase or goblet lost in a shipwreck—
sharp edges smoothed by tumbling waves,
sand, and time; the fragments no longer shiny
but frosted, translucent, mysterious,
their origins transformed, concealed,
essence revealed.

I pick up the pieces and imagine
where they came from—
common white beach glass,
perhaps once a fine milk glass dish;
amber from a bitters bottle,
aqua from electrical insulators,
cobalt blue from a perfume decanter,
sea-foam green from a Coca-Cola bottle;
lavender from glass laced with manganese;
orange, turquoise, and yellow from art glass,
and the rarest—red from a ruby glass goblet
or a sunken ship's lantern.

Tiny windows to the past, they offer a view
of things people carried with them
from faraway places to new homes,
or didn't want anymore and discarded,
now miniature artworks displayed
on a gallery of sand, all fitting
in the palm of my hand.

Oysters Don't Feel Pain

Late April, the last days of the oyster harvest.
He stands at the boat's helm in his stained shirt,
weather-beaten hat, faded blue fishing pants, rubber boots,
steering a slow circle around Copano Bay.
He knows the inner bays, the ebb and flow of tides,
the places where oysters live and multiply and hide.

The trawler drags a basket along the reef,
scraping up oysters. Deckhands dump gray shells on a table,
then sort the oysters by hand—three inches long to be legal.
Some years ago the season ended early; this year it started late
to give the oysters more time to grow. Other years
red tide algae, oil spills, hurricanes killed the harvest.

Go get a construction job, his wife tells him.
We need a bigger house for the kids.

He shakes his head. He likes being his own boss,
promises her the next harvest season will be better.

Papa, do oysters feel pain? his son asks one day as
he shows the boy how to eat a raw oyster.
He takes out his knife, pries open the clasped shell,
frees the glistening flesh with a flash of the blade.
No, oysters don't have a brain, only eyes along the rim.
*When something threatens them, they hide in their shell*s.

The boy shakes his head, refuses to take the oyster.
His father shrugs, swallows it whole.

The days begin at sunrise and end in late afternoon.
He steers the boat to the dock at Fulton Harbor
next to the restaurant where tourists come for the fresh oysters.
They wave from the deck as the men unload the heavy bags.
Tired and sweating, he drives his pickup to the frame house
in the neighborhood that tourists never see.

Go get a construction job, his wife tells him again.
We need a better neighborhood for the kids.

He shakes his head, reminds her he likes being his own boss,
promises her the next harvest season will be better.

There is never enough money, but there is more than enough pain.
He escapes to his boat and enters the world he knows. The first run
dredges a good catch. A stray oyster clatters across the deck.
It looks like a stone, but he feels the life inside the closed shell.
He lifts the oyster to his lips, inhales the sea essence,
and tastes the briny tears.

Ode to a Whooping Crane

We steer the boat into the mouth of Mesquite Bay,
past pink and turquoise condos on the tourist beach

searching for the last flock of Whooping Cranes
at Aransas, marshy melding of land, water, and sky.

True Winter Texans, they arrive each autumn,
migrating from nesting grounds in Canada,

traveling by instinct, calling to each other
with their ancient songs—a whooping *kar-r-r-o-o-o*.

Floating down to forage in warm waters until spring,
they teach their colts to hunt the shallows for blue crabs,

then take flight and head north to their summer place
to mate, build nests, and hatch a new generation.

We raise our binoculars in the morning fog to see
white ghosts on black stilts prowling for prey close to shore,

praying these feathered angels return next year, and the next.
Such grace saves us, too. We are all endangered now.

Haiku: Water and Moon

Isle of wild mustangs—
chasing the ocean, leaving
hoofprints in the sand

Two palms by the bay
lean together like lovers—
kiss the crescent moon

White pelican glides,
hunting above the harbor—
Splash! Fish for dinner

Yellow moon glimmers
like an old Spanish gold coin—
treasure in the sky

She crawls from the sea—
such a big journey to lay
tiny turtle eggs

How swiftly the sun
sets along the laguna
like a ship, sinking

The Hermit Crab Selects a Bigger House

You, so misunderstood, not a hermit or a crab,
but a social crustacean with a soft fleshy tail,

crawl across the sand, dragging your mobile home,
an empty shell discarded by the previous owner,

a snail, now too tight for your expanding torso.
You're in the market for a bigger house,

not a round Whale's Eye this time, but something
roomier. You spy an empty whelk shell, seize it,

pull your curved body out of the Whale's Eye,
wrap yourself into the vacant spiral shell,

only your hard claws and striped legs exposed,
protruding alien eyes, long feelers for fingers,

trying to look fierce as you scavenge the beach for
bits of dead creatures, tiny mussels, clams, algae.

You peel off the rooftop garden of stinging sea anemones,
relocate them to your new shell for a mobile security system.

Behind you in a queue of hermit crabs, the trading up
continues, smaller crabs taking the larger shell in front of it.

We could learn so much from you if we took the time—
you that doesn't expend energy to make something new,

but upcycles a castoff into a castle, fills a vacancy,
finds a place in the world, and makes it yours.

Like a Palm in a Hurricane

The wind screamed like the Furies
coming to seek vengeance,
murdering with a swirling sword,
devouring and regurgitating
pieces of roofs, walls, windows,
proclaiming that life will break you.
Even trees gave up their roots
except for the palms that bent
and bowed to the wind,
roots clinging to soil, refusing to break.

Hiding in my closet, I silently screamed too,
plugging my ears against the shrieking sky
until silence landed with a thud
like the ebony tree on our roof.
I opened the door, peeked outside to see
walls crumbled, glass shattered,
trees uprooted—except for the palm,
beaten but still standing, showing me
to bend the knee of my heart, bow,
cling to life, and never, ever break.

Still Life with Loquats

How often during the summer I escaped
from our noisy house of chattering children
to my South Texas backyard where two loquat trees
grew side by side, their glossy, veined leaves
weaving a tarpaulin so thick that grass
could not grow underneath, but I could,
spending hours daydreaming, reading,
or just being still.

Under the loquat trees I listened
to the woodpeckers' rat-a-tat-tatting,
to sprinklers hissing in the neighbor's yard,
to the low murmur of bees,
to mockingbirds chirping in the trees,
mobbing the clusters of tart-sweet loquats
also called Japanese plums, tough to peel
but such an exotic tropical flavor
like a drop of sunshine on my tongue.
I learned loquats were native to China,
then raised in Japan for a thousand years.
They transported me to faraway places
beyond the redwood fence that formed
the border of my sheltered life.

Decades later when I visited Japan,
I saw a painting in a gallery—
a tiny mountain bird perched
on a loquat branch with a cluster of fruit.
I felt such longing for that cool shade,
those tangy-sweet drops of sunshine,
and mostly, that stillness.

Midnight in the Greenhouse of Desire

Last night we were just going to admire
orchids in the moonlight.
In the greenhouse the moist air
felt heavy with longing.
A kiss led to another and then more.

Their bright faces watched us so intently,
exposing their voluptuous petals,
their quivering ruffled lips and sticky tongues
designed for pollination, male and female in one flower,
desiring of at least a threesome.

They open themselves to discovery
by tiny feet and hairy bodies
probing, groping, searching
their secret places, fulfilling their
one true purpose—to be touched.

I closed my eyes, felt breath and skin
against me as the orchids nodded their blessing,
my back pressed against the wooden table
where I'd gently pushed the pots aside
and felt their earthy dampness.

I opened my eyes, saw his face above mine,
not adoring but indifferent, then felt a rush
of regret. I left the orchids in the moonlight
luring their suitors—a bee, a moth, an ant—
with deliberate intent and no regrets, ever.

How I envy them, blooming day and night,
their beauty fresh and glistening,
worshipped in their house of water and light,
their desire satisfied while tonight
I will be alone in my house, petals dry, untouched.

Thirsting

I dreamed of
a place by the water
white curtains
breeze blowing across
the sea, white clouds
sailing like galleons
a cottage with shutters
cats sunning on the porch
a small boat for fishing
you by my side
at high and low tides
never thirsting
for water
always thirsting
for more

You dreamed of
a place in the desert
turquoise doors
hot days, cool nights
sagebrush and cacti
wrens nesting in thorns
an adobe with vigas
dogs running in theyard
a backpack for hiking
solitude and coyotes
for company at night
always thirsting
for water
never thirsting
for more

Like Foam on the Water

My memories come in flashes,
in old photos with round corners,
in faded snapshots without borders—
pictures drift in my mind
like foam on the water.

My backyard in summer:
red bathing suit, sprinkler hissing,
butterflies dancing, parents kissing,
thinking everything is all right,
looking happy for the camera.

My bedroom at midnight:
dark walls, moonlight daggers,
loud voices, glass shatters.
I pull the covers over my head,
pretend I'm in a tent in a forest.

Our kitchen, next morning:
yellow sunflowers, blue door,
broken china on the floor—
someone forgot to sweep,
hide the shards in the trash.

My bathroom, later afternoon:
I close the door, retreat,
pink rug soft beneath my feet.
Turn on the faucet, fill the tub—
bubbles help me forget.

Years later, back home:
I walk alone by the bay,
release my mind from yesterday,
let the pictures drift away
like white foam on gray water.

Castaway at Midnight

Is anybody out there?
I typed into the blue glow,
hurling my message in a bottle
into dark water.

Yes, I'm here, someone answered.
Where are you?
I don't know.
I'm here, too, wrote another.
How are you?
I don't know, but I'm glad you're there.

Letters on the screen blink
like lights on the horizon,
boats searching for a harbor
and landing on my island.

The Nautilus Heart

Pearly, secret chambers pump seawater
in, out, in, out, so the nautilus
can swim without tail or fins,
propelled through life
by a heart beating in a hard shell,
unbreakable.

Ancient Greeks saw perfection
in the divine design—
logarithmic spiral,
Dürer's "eternal line,"
like a hurricane, a galaxy,
the way a hawk circles prey.

Those who seek perfection
often destroy it, desiring the nautilus
for its nacre, hard and iridescent,
perfect for cheap jewelry,
or for the entire shell, to display
like a piece of priceless art.

A living fossil survived extinction
in the sea only to face
the ultimate predator on land,
propelled through life
by a multi-chambered heart
beating in a hard shell,
broken.

At Padre Island

Father's Day, 2016

She's only been gone a month
but it feels longer than that.
He needs to get out of the house,
my sister and I agree.
Dad, where would you like to go?
Padre Island, he says.

We drive thirty minutes from Corpus Christi
over the high curve of causeway to the island
named for Padre Ballí, a Spanish missionary priest.
Our father doesn't want to go to the county park
with its picnic tables and fishing pier.
Too many people. Too many memories.

We drive farther down the island to Malaquite,
from the Spanish word *malaquita* for green malachite.
The water is clear there, the color of a cat's eyes.
We park in the lot, follow the boardwalk
to the pavilion, sit on a bench in the shade.
Seagulls circle us, squawking.

He stares at the Gulf, not saying much.
Dunes frame the view of water and lapping waves.
He used to bring her to Padre Island even though
he didn't like the wind, salt, sand in the car.
She fed popcorn to the gulls, tossing pieces in the air,
laughing as they swooped to get a bite.

He wants to buy a shell in the gift shop,
a Lightning Whelk, her favorite, holds it up to his ear.
That's all he wants for Father's Day, to hear the sea,
the echo of her laughter. I tell him she would love
that we came out here. He looks out at the waves,
nods, tucks the shell in his pocket.

The Closing

I walked through my childhood home
for the last time with a stranger who
bought it at a cheap price to resell
to other people I will never know.
It felt like a tomb of a house,
dead without any people living
in the rooms. The new owner said it needs
a new roof, plumbing, electrical work,
old carpet ripped up, tile replaced.
Mainly it needs more joy, fewer tears.

I took the brass key off the metal ring,
the key that unlocked the door
when I tiptoed in after midnight
when I was supposed to be in by eleven;
the key I duplicated so I could let myself in
when my dying father was too ill to open the door,
the key that meant I had two homes even
after I married, that I was still someone's child.

Now an orphan handed the key to the stranger.
He put it in a lockbox, hung it on the doorknob
so other strangers could cross the threshold.
I stood there on the porch steps, thought I glimpsed a face
but there was no one at the window.
Only the elm tree in the front yard
waved its branches at me.

There was no one to tell goodbye.
I got in my car, put it in reverse, paused,
took a breath. Then I raised the invisible anchor,
backed out of the driveway into what used to be
my street, and watched my childhood
fade away in the rear-view mirror.

To My Father's Orchids

Tell me,
please tell me what he did
to make you bloom,
to convince you to send up a flower spike,
to open your buds and reveal such splendor,
to make your roots crawl out of their pots,
to dangle like fingers reaching for the light.
Whisper the secrets you told him about beauty
so he never lost faith you would bloom again.
Turn your faces to me—some flat, some with a ruffled lip,
some with fringed petals, some striped, some spotted—
tell me how you all came to thrive in this place
and bloom—bloom!—for him but not for me.
You do not have any choice now, do you understand?
He is gone and not coming back, your caretaker, your god.
He left all of you to me, despite—perhaps because of—
my shortcomings, so I would have something to tend.
Now your fleshy green leaves sag—are you grieving as I am?
Take heart that he loved you like children,
showered on you his time and energy and devotion.
Now I really need to know: What makes you bloom?
Can you please, please, please
tell me?

Chrysalis

I lie here in the darkness
Waiting, wondering
If I'm in a coffin
If I will ever see light
If I will die here, suffocating

Then I feel the stirring within
A dry raspy rustling
And I burst forth
Transformed
Unfolding new wings

They bear me upward, outward
Toward flowers and sweet nectar
Food for my journey
For my metamorphosis into
Another realm, all air and light

An Orchid's Guide to Life

Do not put me in the ground
like a common dirt plant.

My roots will suffocate or drown;
they must breathe.

Look up, in the trees' branches
trembling in the wind

or on a cliff wall—
see how my roots dangle, free.

I am there, bearing witness
to creatures stirring down below,

born in the coolness, dying in the sun
like ocean fog or desert rain.

You fear the unknown, but I know
how to live in wet or dry places.

I take sustenance from the air,
rain, sun, tree bark, forest floor,

adapting to change, clinging to life,
blooming because it's my nature.

II.

Arid Places

Ancestral

they dance in a canyon

    creators of their own songs

        drums beating in rhythm

            and every god listened

beneath the full buck moon

    reflected in the mirror-river

        their star-eyes watching

            breath of galaxies upon them

becoming part of the infinite stream

    sound and light and heat

        the pulse of the universe

Rocks of Ages

I pray in Notre Dame below flying buttresses,
kneel by dead poets at Westminster Abbey,
make a pilgrimage to Dante's tomb in Ravenna,
light a candle in the Ranchos church Georgia O'Keeffe painted,
all transcending stone and brick, mud and glass,

yet none so sacred to me as cathedrals of rock
at Chaco, Santa Elena, Palo Duro, Monument Valley,
sanctuaries carved by water, wind, time,
evidence of a force greater than humankind,
buttresses of sandstone arches, dome of turquoise sky.

I genuflect at the altar of beauty and truth,
worship within soaring walls of infinite grains of sand,
baptized in waters of rivers and creeks,
canyons awash in patterns of light more colorful
than any manmade stained-glass windows,

inner sanctum presided over not by angels
but by creatures chirping, howling, singing like a choir,
glorifying creation with no religion except nature,
measuring eternity with the seasons and the
constant churning of sun, moon, and stars.

One Day in Santa Fe

Only one, when my young father, chasing my mother,
who had spirited me away from California,
homesick for her Texas home, stopped in
Santa Fe. He fell in love with adobe walls
standing for centuries, turquoise sky,
silver streams, strings of red chiles hanging
by roadsides, blue corn tortillas, and the light,
the light that clarified everything.

He longed to stay, but he kept driving to Texas,
staying there for sixty years in a place he hated for love.
Now I am driving through Tucumcari, turning north
onto the road that cuts north through red canyonlands,
past roadside memorials for the dead, my father's spirit
in the passenger seat, returning to Santa Fe
to stay for more than one day so I can see the light,
the light that clarifies everything.

In an Arid Place

If grief were a landscape
it would look like
a desert canyon where
I saw spring water dripping
down a stone wall,
trailing dark streaks
like tracks of dirty tears.
How could so little water
make much difference
in such an arid place,
I wondered, but then I looked up
and saw hanging gardens—
moss and ferns sprouting
from rock crevices, lush spots
of green against brown,
dangling hope that love could
take root again in my arid heart.

Vessel

Lonnie Vigil made
a pot it won at
Indian Market
in Santa Fe a few years
back strange because it was
black no decoration only black
as night with stars suspended in the
clay flecks of mica to give it light give it
spirit that pot glittered and burned with a fire
from deep inside even though you could not see it
could not touch it but could feel it they say that vessels
are the containers of the soul long ago the ancient people
placed vessels over the faces of the dead and buried them
now grave robbers dig up the pots and leave the ancient
bones to bleach white in the desert they steal the souls
and they will come to great evil it is said I believe it
because a vessel is like a human form with a neck
and a belly and a foot and a spirit and a voice
and the echo of that voice is called beauty a
vessel transformed by human hands out
of clay from the bones of the dead
now part of the earth I looked
inside Lonnie's pot to see
whose soul was there
in the bottom was
a hot ember
burning
still

Ode on an Acoma Pot

After John Keats' "Ode on a Grecian Urn"

What a thing of beauty is an Acoma pot,
vessel of the desert molded from local clay
dug from a secret place around Acoma,
enchanted mesa west of Albuquerque where
Pueblo people live as they have for centuries.
The Spanish could not conquer them, nor could other foes.
The people have lived there now for two thousand years,
holding their love of beauty close to their hearts.

Potters breathed life into the lump of gray,
rolling ropes of clay, coiling each layer,
building the pot's walls and scraping them thin
with a piece of dried gourd, hoarding patience,
burnishing the urn with a polishing stone,
until it feels as smooth as fine porcelain,
then firing the pot on a pyre of dried dung.
From the ashes rises a pot pure and white as bone.

The artist takes her brush made of yucca spikes
to paint thin black lines, depicting the world in
geometric designs on vases, bowls, hanging canteens.
She tells stories of land, people, universe
with triangles, spirals, stairsteps to the sky—
symbols of the pueblo's most sacred scenes,
art that has endured all these centuries.
The pots become vessels that hold the old souls.

A gallery in Santa Fe—on Canyon Road, no less—
sold Acoma pots by Lucy Lewis and Marie Chino.
Their artistry was plain to see, but the pot
that beguiled me most was made by Juana Leno—
a triple canteen joined by braided clay handles,
black spirals entwining with no visible ends.
Hear it call without any words spoken as
the vessel leaves its form and truth ascends.

O'Keeffe's House

West of Santa Fe, I drive into the landscape
of Technicolor-striped cliffs and twisted hoodoos,
past red mesas and dark canyons to Abiquiu,
a village near Ghost Ranch.
I park in front of a rambling adobe,
low walls enclosing a garden,
walk past the black patio door,
the square step stones I saw in paintings,
cross the threshold of Georgia O'Keeffe's house,
feel the summer air change from hot to cool
within thick adobe walls smoothed by hands,
muslin curtains wafting in the kitchen window,
nichos holding miniature still lifes
of simple things she collected—
bones, shells, horns, stones
that spoke to her of the desert beyond:
the delicate skeleton of a coiled rattlesnake
preserved under glass like sculpture,
giant window framing the arid panorama
anchored by the blue anvil mountain,
the Pedernal. She once said that God told her
if she painted it enough, He would give it her.
I look at the Pedernal towering above the valley,
stark and silent and shimmering in sunlight,
and feel her there, in the place that is now hers.

The Last Painter on Earth

After James Doolin's painting of the same name.

Hiking in the desert, I came upon
the Last Painter on Earth, standing
at his easel, brush in hand, painting
a landscape of red rock and pink sand,
the sky impossibly blue. "Why are you
out here all alone?" I asked. "I'm here
for the same reason you are," he replied.
"To find out what is true."

I continued down the trail and when I looked back
the tubes of paint had spilled from his pack;
he stood at his easel like a statue.
Arms uplifted, his shadow reached to the clouds
on the canvas he had painted en plein air;
rocks stacked to the moon like a giant red stair,
the sky impossibly blue.

Conquistador

The piñon trees saw who did it.
An amputation without blood,
a severing without screams.
Some called it an act of defiance.
Rebellion. A reckoning.
Others shook their heads.
Bad luck to stir up old ghosts.

A bronze foot in a spurred boot,
sawed off one December night
two dozen years ago in Alcalde,
New Mexico, from the statue of
Don Juan de Oñate. The thief hid it
like a treasure, one with no value
except to those who knew.

Oñate, despot, conquistador,
cut toes off prisoners. Should he not
suffer the same fate symbolically?
Someone painted the left foot red,
wrote the words "Remember 1680,"
year of the Pueblo revolt. At Acoma,
they tossed Spaniards over the cliffs.

The legacy of conquest runs long, deep,
red. Longstanding resentments simmer,
embers of revolt never extinguished.
Oñate's statue on horseback, new foot
welded on, looks whole again but
the piñon trees saw it all. They know.
He did not conquer anyone.

Haiku: Desert Colors

The sun bakes the land.
Silver lake glimmers. I dive
into the mirage

White bones lie gleaming
on red rock carved by dry wind—
skeletons of time

River of gray stones
silent in summer's embrace—
hear it scream for rain

Evening on the rim,
yellow glow in the distance—
a faraway ranch

Ivory moon hung
on an ebony tree branch—
clouds caught on the thorns

Two Crows in a Canyon

two black crows flap their wings

    above a silver river slithering

        caws echoing down the canyon

           as they shoot like dark arrows

        across the abyss, alight on the edge

    then throw themselves

back into the wind again

At Elephant Tusk

A memory: four friends, topographical map in hand,
compass, provisions stuffed in our backpacks,

disappearing into the desert out in Big Bend,
hiking single file on a faint trail through

sparse lechugilla and creosote, guided by cairns,
walking through dust and time, trying not to lose our way.

Back at crowded Panther Junction, the ranger asked
where we wanted to go. Wherever no one else is going,

we told him. Two hours later, after bumping over dirt roads,
we arrived at the trailhead pointing us to Elephant Tusk,

volcanic pinnacle thirty million years old, jutting
above the desert floor, remote and primitive.

No trees or shade, no toilets, no amenities except
solitude and sky. Nothing and everything we needed.

We pitched our dome tents on a rocky point so high
we could almost lasso the half moon rising that night

above the ivory outline of Elephant Tusk,
mammoth pedestal holding up the fire-ice firmament.

We, such tiny figures in a boundless landscape,
felt our human insignificance and reveled in it.

Ode to a Pair of Worn-Out Hiking Boots

I remember the day I bought them,
more expensive than any shoes I owned,
purchased for a special mission – to hike
from the top to the bottom of the Grand Canyon.
Tan suede and dark blue waterproof Gortex fabric,
red striped laces, sturdy sole that hugged my feet,
they bore me down to Phantom Ranch and back up
the Bright Angel Trail to the South Rim.

Other canyons beckoned—in Texas, Palo Duro,
Caprock, Santa Elena Canyon in Big Bend,
four days of backpacking at Elephant Tusk;
in the Arizona wilderness, Aravaipa Canyon,
cliff faces crawling with chattering coatimundis,
no trail to follow except in the creek, holding
backpacks above our heads, hiking boots
propelling me through the water. I thought
they would fall apart after that, but they dried out
and acted as if nothing had happened.

The boots bore me on trails for another twenty years,
old friends with stories of deserts traversed,
mountains climbed, more rivers crossed,
looking no worse for the wear.
Then one hot day in June, on a rocky trail
in the Davis Mountains, one of the soles fell off.
I trudged on, pebbles working their way into my socks.
At the trail's end, the other sole came off,
glue finally weakened. They lay in the dust,
artifacts of adventure.

I bought a new pair of hiking boots,
same brand, different color—tan and turquoise,
even a few bucks cheaper. Same sturdy sole, snug fit,
no blisters on their first outing on steep trails
in the Rocky Mountains outside Durango.
They became new friends, but I miss the old ones
that offered so much support. When I was teetering
on the edge of an abyss, they saved me.
They lie together in a box like yin and yang relics,
reminders to keep trudging up mountains and
down into canyons lest my soul end up in a box,
too, forever closed.

Desperado in Palo Duro

Written in November 2020 after I had recovered from COVID.

If I could run away, where would I go?
I know....

Driving the long road from Canyon to Palo Duro,
I check my rearview mirror, feeling like I'm on the lam.

Nothing in sight except for land and sky. Nothing much
in any direction except a lone windmill drumming

the wind, pumping water into a concrete trough mobbed
by cattle with no tree for cover, no shelter in sight.

The Llano Estacado feels like a rectangle so flat
you can see the edges. Then the crack begins

in the tabletop. With every mile it yawns wider and
deeper and redder until the Earth exposes its insides.

I drive toward the abyss, register at the state park station,
get my campsite number, and drive down, down, down

into millions of years. Hoodoos like lighthouses stand
like beacons carved and sculpted by wind and water.

The sinking sun throws darts of fire into the violet
descending. Cattle move along the rim like ebony ghosts.

The ivory moon rises, clouds caught on the mesquite thorns.
I pitch my tent, eat some slices of cheese, crackers, and grapes,

wash them down with a camp cup of wine, watch the electric sky.
There goes a silver-tailed star falling into the nothingness. I crawl

inside the tent, unroll my sleeping bag, and lie on my back,
listening to the echoes of time and the coyotes' refrain—

a howl from the bowels of black space. They sound like the dogs
of mythical hunter Orion, placed among the stars by Zeus.

The sun peeks over the rim. A woodpecker awakens me,
squawking from the top of a dead mesquite tree. Another day,

another chance to outrun the invisible demon. Surely it cannot find me
at the bottom of Palo Duro. If it does, no place is safe.

Eggs bubble in a pan on my camp stove. Shadows move
on the ground. Buzzards—nature's dark angels—circle

above in the big blue sky. I point at them with my fork.
"You ain't gettin' me," I tell them. "Not just yet."

Walking the Paluxy River in Drought

In summer I like to walk upstream on the Paluxy
to see its dry riverbed gleaming white in the sun,
limestone wavy from millennia of flowing water.

If I keep walking, I will spot them: records scattered
of those who came before me 113 million years ago
when giants walked on the edge of an ancient ocean.

In wet years, the triangular tracks made by
a three-toed dinosaur called Acrocanthosaurus
lie beneath the Paluxy's shallow waters, barely visible.

In dry years, the tracks hold water like puddles, then
the water evaporates, revealing toes and claws captured
in motion—right foot, left foot, right foot, left foot.

Other Texas rivers depend on water for their power,
but drought transforms the Paluxy from insignificant to epic,
exposing its natural history museum under a vast roof of sky.

As I walk the dry streambed, I try to envision
fifteen-foot-tall, seven-ton creatures trudging here,
their size and weight sinking tracks deep in mud.

A shallow pool beckons me to remove my shoes,
feel cool mud squish between my toes. I walk onward,
leaving no impression, no record that I was ever here.

As Long As Birds Fly Without Borders

they will survive, free.
What if they had to land at a check station,
show their IDs,
declare what they're carrying—nothing—
then wait for the okay to take off again?
Would they have to apply for asylum,
then wait in a makeshift camp for weeks or months?

What if they had to carry a passport
for every country they entered and exited?
What if they could not land in a storm
to find shelter, alight to search for food,
find a mate, build a nest, lay eggs,
raise chicks? Migrate spring and fall,
as their instincts direct them year after year?

As long as we cannot live without borders,
we will not survive, free.

Wild Horse Desert

Clouds billow like sails of Spanish galleons
above the *brasada*, silver-green thicket, tangle
of sage, mesquite, prickly pear cactus, land between
the Rio Grande and Nueces River. Some call it
the Texas "brush country," others the Wild Horse Desert.

Its native people did not want or need the Spanish
to discover, convert, or conquer them.
They ground bitter mesquite beans into flour
while blood soaked into soil, ran into rivers.
The conquistadors never found gold, only resistance.

Their galleons brought horses that escaped, multiplied,
galloped in wild herds across the arid landscape,
a million of them at one point, more horses than people,
so many horses it looked like the ground was moving,
so many they all could not be captured.

Spanish descendants cross the Rio Grande again,
escaping like wild horses, roaming the *brasada*
in search of treasure—a new homeland. They find
mostly resistance, parched ground, rattlesnakes,
thorns, thirst, coyotes on four legs and two legs.

So many come now, are captured, corralled, sent back.
They leave tracks in the sand, empty water bottles,
sun-bleached bones scattered on cracked earth.
The wild horses have all but disappeared—
vanished into the desert, but never captured, never tamed.

Rattled

A stick in the road moves
as my boots crunch on gravel;
diamonds on the back, dark bands
around the tail. Not a stick after all.

I feel for the pistol in my pocket,
loaded with ratshot, pull it out,
take off the safety, finger the trigger,
the metal as cold as a snake's scales.

The triangular head raises up,
eyes with slits for irises,
forked red tongue flicking at me,
tasting the air, tasting me.

The snake coils. I recoil.
Rattles shake, hissing like a deep fryer.
I get the message: "Go away,
human. You're too big to eat."

I have the snake in the crosshairs.
My instinct kicks in: "Kill it."
I imagine the boom, pointy head
flying off, body writhing on the ground.

I put the gun away, pick up a stone,
hurl it. The serpent strikes at it,
then slithers under a cedar tree.
My instinct lies dead in the gravel.

Horns and Bones

They whisper to me
as I walk in the desert—
sun-bleached skulls
of horses, cows, coyotes,
sanded by wind and time,
scattered on red earth:
clavicles and jawbones,
leg bones and ribs,
a pelvis like a saddle tree—
O'Keeffe held it up to the sky,
painted the empty socket blue,
then red with yellow
like a portal to the universe.
I gather shed antlers from deer,
horns of goats and audads
killed by cars or coyotes
or some other predator,
leave them on an ant bed,
let nature strip flesh from bone
so I can see the underlying structure,
the evidence in my hands
that life and death are
the front and back of reality.

Ode to a Sunflower

This is how you began—
stardust that fell to Earth
becoming black seeds buried,
waiting for rain, warmth, rebirth;
prickly stalk reaching skyward,
unbending; flower a tiny sun
awakening, following her mother
journeying from east to west,
vanishing below the horizon.

You are the daughter of stars,
brown-eyed, yellow-haired goddess,
eye-dazzling against blue sky;
Helios Anthos, symbol of loyalty,
longevity, adoration. You endure
heat and drought but open yourself
to beauty. Even as invaders attack,
trying to pry you from the land,
you stand tall, roots clinging to soil.

Light reveals you are not one flower
but many, tiny florets surrounded
by golden petals like sun rays,
seeds arranged in Fibonacci spirals,
portrait of nature's perfection.
You defeat invaders by never dying,
your seed carried by birds or wind,
gilding fields, meadows, hillsides,
beginning anew, following the sun.

Resurrection

Dead, dried snake lies in the dust
on a gravel road outside Santa Fe,

flattened by car wheels, stiff as old leather;
it speaks to me, not with a hiss but a whisper.

I came to New Mexico to paint adobe churches,
not a desiccated serpent;

translucent skin and delicate bones curving
in a frozen "S," the flesh lost forever.

I lay the carcass on a flat rock, take a pencil
from my bag, cover the remains with white paper,

rub soft gray lead back and forth
as I have done on my ancestors' tombstones.

Spine and scales weave a raised pattern,
a ghost image that crawls across the page,

then drops to the ground and slithers away,
leaving its silver spirit on my hands.

Spiral World

With the tip of my pen
I draw a point on a blank page,
then a circle, unclosed.
A silent force takes my hand,
and the pen goes around and around
until I'm inside a fiddlehead fern unfurling,
a snail winding into a fragile shell,
water spinning in a whirlpool,
a dust devil skipping across the desert,
a hurricane pirouetting into the Gulf.

At Mesa Verde, ancestral Puebloans
painted Tularosa swirls in black and white
on the bellies of clay pots.
Ancient ones in the desert Southwest
carved spirals into stone.
In Texas, Tonkawa women painted
concentric circles on their bare breasts.
Sacred symbol, secret key
unlocking universal truths,
corkscrewing in and out of time,
orbiting with planets around stars,
swirling with galaxies into the celestial soup,
uncovering the passage from inner to outer,
human to divine.

There's no beginning, no end,
to this spiral world, only
an eternal coiling and uncoiling,
an infinite spool winding and unwinding.
Death is but an entry point into the force
that spins forever and that exists
for a few moments on a blank page
that I hold in my hand.

III.

Places of Shelter

The Art of Stillness

The Italians call it *il dolce far niente*—
      the sweetness of doing nothing.
Be still and hear the wind
      whispering in the juniper
Stop and listen to the sounds of lizards
      skittering in the leaves.
Sit and observe the Queens and Monarchs
      flitting among mistflowers, sipping nectar.
See how bushes bloom with sanguine roses,
      admiring the red ooze from the thorn prick.
Watch how bees wriggle between petals,
      searching for the sweet spot.
Look, really look, at the sunflower
      spiraling in Fibonacci perfection.
Touch the hairy stem, feel the silent pulse
      transforming sunlight into sustenance.

This is how to create a masterpiece
      never seen in a museum or a gallery,
curated in the beating heart,
      transforming stillness into art.

Alighting

My sanctuary is a land of juniper-oak woodlands,
home of cardinals, chickadees, woodpeckers,
titmice, wrens, crows, juncos. Each morning
they chirp and squawk, beseeching me
to fill feeders with black oil sunflower seeds,
the rock pond with water. Birds flutter down
like angels of a greater god. I feed them and
they feed me. They take refuge, here.

Endangered Golden-cheeked Warblers arrive
each spring, flashing their bright yellow faces.
They fly over mountains, migrate free of borders,
settle in this pocket of Texas, the only place
on Earth where they nest. Tiny beaks weave
strips of cedar bark with spider webs for cradles,
lay three or four eggs, one clutch a season.
Instinct makes a stand against extinction.

This sanctuary was theirs long before I came.
How did we, different species of the same universe,
choose this place to alight? I watch warblers flit
between live oak branches, pecking at insects
hidden in lichens. They dip their beaks in water,
gold cheeks glowing against gray rock, then fly
back into the woods. I cannot touch them, but I feel
their wild hearts beating. I take refuge, there.

Notched Horizon

The sun sets above Chalk Mountain, not
a mountain at all, but a long limestone mesa,

nothing out there but a ghost town on the edge,
some ranch houses, a bar, a Masonic lodge.

From our ridge looking west, the blue mountain
with a chunk whittled out—a gap, a notch—

measures time and the seasons. The sun crawls along
the notched horizon, sinking to the north in summer,

then creeping south all autumn. Around the winter solstice,
it finally rests its head in the notch, then vanishes.

For a while the notch looks empty, but then
coyotes howl as the waxing crescent moon rises,

hanging in the sky like a silver reaping hook,
harvesting the last rays of light.

The Shelter of Place

We call it the Middle of Nowhere,
the Beautiful Oblivion, or just "the ranch"—
one hundred twenty-two acres or so,
mostly limestone ledges, hills consumed
by mountain cedar and prickly pear,
crawling with rattlesnakes and fire ants,
enough pasture and two stock ponds
to raise Texas Longhorns, a couple of
Quarter horses, a pair of donkeys.
Eight miles south of the nearest town,
a mile off the highway,
a gravel road bumping, winding,
dipping, climbing to a ridgetop.

Why do you want to live way out there,
city friends asked when we moved here.
No neighbors to help you, no cafes, no bars,
no cinema, no concerts, nothing to do.
You're lucky to live way out there
they say in the post-pandemic world.
No neighbors to infect you, no crowds,
plus the biggest luxury—space.
We hear the fear in their voices with
each outbreak, afraid of what they see
and what they cannot as they take shelter,
working from home, often feeling lonely or
trapped living in a big city.

We knew that life and abandoned it. Now we
work from home, too. It leaves more time
to hunt fossils on our ancient beach
or watch the aerial jousting of hummingbirds
around flutes of red yucca blooms on long spikes.
What would it be like not to see the sky,
or witness the ritual of dawn and dusk,
sun catching clouds on fire, night
extinguishing them before flipping a switch
to turn on lights in the heavens.
We take solace from this chaotic world in
Nature's order as we shelter—in place.

Stony Path

I could have trod up the gravel road
after feeding the horses this morning;

instead, I took the stony path up the hill
to trace the patterns of long morning shadows

to listen to dried grass whisper to the wind,
to feel feathery seedheads tickle my legs,

to notice wispy clouds caressing cerulean sky,
to sense the season changing, and I am part of it all,

a sojourner in this wild perfection
gathering moments of peace.

Walking Through Time

I hike into the limestone hills
after an afternoon rain washed away
the dust, the sun's low angle
highlighting shadows and textures.

My shoes crunch on the gravel and
I step on something hard, bend down
to look, spot a spiral half-embedded in rock.
A gastropod—a common snail.

This ancient beach left a record of
two hundred million years—
puffed urchins called echinoids,
red and yellow coral, scallop shells,

oyster shells shaped like gray ears,
heart-shaped clams, underwater lily
stems, once delicate, now hard and ringed,
dark chunks of metal from meteorites.

I gather them in buckets, lug them home
to place in boxes and on windowsills,
in a wooden bread bowl full now
of cold Cretaceous sculptures.

Nature replaced delicate flesh
that once lived inside the shells,
filling the molds with silt and mud,
hardening them with pressure and time.

When the ancient seas and rivers receded,
they lay there for millennia under the stars
until I walked by, picked up a fossil, and
held immortality in my hand.

Haiku: Texas Moon

Blue moon at Marfa,
mystery lights in the desert—
cosmic cowboys ride

Palo Duro moon
shines high above the canyon—
lamp for the Lighthouse

Moon on the Brazos:
canoeing by candlelight
down a blue river

In the river's bend
moon hangs above the Chisos
telling ghost stories

Blood moon on the rise,
shadows on the Seven Knobs—
crimson and cedar

Coyotes in Moonlight

I never see you in daylight,
but I know you're out there in the dark.
I hear you howling at midnight,
imagine you running through tall grass,
hunger, thirst, the search for a mate driving you
over hills, through woods, across creeks.
You run so fast and hard, then lie down,
nose to tail, to rest until night falls,
when the moon throws icy blue daggers
and the hunger and howling begin again.

I envy your animal heart, never questioning,
second-guessing, obsessing, regretting,
as I stand here on a ridge and listen
to your yowls echo across black space,
yearning to run free with you,
yellow eyes trained for night vision,
chasing, pouncing, killing prey, feeding pups,
fulfilling what you were born to do,
while I stand here alone on my hill,
howling in my human heart.

Four Legs Flying

Chasing cloud shadows or nothing at all,
silver tail trailing like stardust on a comet,
he runs because he can, because he was designed to,
four legs cycling like a wheel in a flying gallop,
not touching the ground at times in stride
as Eadweard Muybridge's photos proved
to doubters more than a century ago.

I named him Stardust Sky Dancer,
almost black when he was born, then faded to grulla
scattered with white hairs, then finally all white,
like night turning into day, Helios and Erebus entwined,
Pegasus flying across a Texas ranch,
galloping across the pasture to greet me,
nickering, snorting, neighing.

He appears in a dust cloud, comes to an abrupt halt,
waits at the corral gate. Dark glassy eyes look into mine,
soft muzzle nuzzles my cheek. It's morning and
he's hungry. I dump oats into a metal feeder;
he sweeps them up with his wide pink tongue,
wanders into the pasture, looks back at me
as if to say, "Aren't you coming?"

I buckle on the saddle, climb on his back,
give him free rein to run. As he streaks
to the horizon, I close my eyes and imagine us
soaring into the sky like the Flying Horse of Gansu,
ancient and new, delicate and strong, wind and fire.
When I open my eyes, we are back on solid ground,
Stardust grazing on tender grass, wings folded.

An acrostic golden shovel merges two forms. In acrostic poems, the first letter in each line spells a word or phrase. In this poem, the phrase is "Give me your tired, your poor, your huddled masses." In golden shovels, the last word in each line is borrowed from an existing work, often a poem or song. In this poem, the last word in each line is the end of the bronze plaque inscription and date on the Statue of Liberty from the poem "The New Colossus" by Emma Lazarus.

Yearning to Breathe Free

Go out into the wildness, my friend, and give
Into your desire to lose yourself with me
Validate your existence, discover your
Embedded strength; do not give up when tired
Make yourself forge ahead, focus your
Eyes on the riches, remembering when you were poor
Young, and restless, determined to set out on your
Own; remember that your ancestors in caves huddled
Unaware that someday there would be such masses
Running amok, and cities, and technology, and still a yearning
To return to places with no cellphones and computers, to
Immerse the spirit in nature, to find places where you can breathe
Releasing the heart longing to soar, to be free
Embracing the sky, floating on ravens' wings into the
Dawn filling the canyon, where the wretched
Yowling ceases and the rotting refuse
Of alleyways and streets disappears like a bad dream of
Urban blight crushing you; throw open your
Room's windows, unleash the restless spirit teeming
Paddle a canoe down a river, ride a wave upon the shore
Or toss a message in a bottle to send
Over oceans proclaiming that you have discovered these
Rocks of ancient ages, handprints on cave walls, the
Ying and yang, a place of refuge where you will never be homeless
Or hopeless, cast away on an island like a boat, tempest-tost
Unfurl your passion to discover the heartland, to
Rest your weariness on my wings and fly with me,
Hanging on to your desires and not falling, for it is I
Unafraid to bear you across the vast spaces and lift
Darkness like the drapes of my robe, my
Dreams for you burning like a glowing lamp
Lighting your way, skirting the shadows beside
Eden's tent, following the path, marking the
Distance to the crystal shoreline, the sun's reflection so golden
Melting into the water, the rays holding open the door
America, seek out the worthy and righteous again—
Say the name that means whole and universal, Emma
Say the name that means dead and resurrected, Lazarus
Enter the canyon, climb the mountain, open your arms every November
Stand like a statue with a torch, shouting those words from 1883

Insomnia

Be still, my unquiet mind;
don't go down that dark hallway,
doors on each side half-open,
beckoning me to enter
rooms with faces floating in the wallpaper.
Echoes and creaks and a stifled scream—
I have been there too many times.

I close my eyes, pray for sleep.
Outside the moon slides below the clouds,
throws a dagger of light across my face.
My eyes flutter open; I look out the window.
A creature rustles in the garden;
irises sway like violet ghosts.
I toss back the covers.

It's coming.

I get up, go to the kitchen, pour a glass of water.
An invisible icy hand rests on my shoulder;
I shudder and wrap myself in a robe.
The clock ticks, the pendulum swings,
the kitchen faucet drips and so does my mind,
counting off the things I must do tomorrow
but tomorrow is already today.

I surrender and retreat to bed.
The moon sets, the rays no longer pierce my pillow.
Doors close, faces fade into the wallpaper.
I fall into a deep sleep and dream...
Artists paint naked people in a strange room;
spies chase me with guns; I'm sick in a hospital.
I run to the edge of an abyss and start falling, falling, falling...

I jolt awake, soaked with sweat,
relieved to see sunlight and a brief reprieve
until the afternoon shadows lengthen,
the carousel begins spinning in my head,
horses frozen in gallop, nostrils flared,
chasing each other around in circles.
I hold on, eyes shut, but I do not sleep.

Murmuration

We swarm
    a flock of individuals
        a collective with no leader
            aligning with no rhyme
                revolving with no reason
            pulsating like a heartbeat
    whirling like a sprite in flight

We do not touch
    or collide but ripple like a wave
        float like a vessel on a current
            sail like a kite on a river of wind

They ask
    whether it's intelligence or instinct
        they study how we should behave
            employ their algorithms
                their models and theories but
        they do not begin to explain us

We express
    our nature, our winged joy together
        yet apart, defying logic, predictability
    geese fly in V-formation

We fly
    in swirls that start   and stop   and start again
        drawing arabesques in the sky
            ebbing, flowing
                in the ocean of air
        then
We disappear
    like a black star
        no sound but the beating of
            a thousand wings
        mingling into
    a murmur

Rhapsody in Bluebonnets

Pebbly seeds tossed on barren ground
in the fall, trusting rain and sun to hatch
star-shaped leaves arranged in rosettes,
lying in wait all winter, cloaked in frost,
stirring with spring's awakening,
stretching for Gershwin's glissando notes,
becoming the state flower, *Lupinus texensis*,
cobalt blue rhapsody under cerulean sky,
florets like the miniature sunbonnets
pioneer women wore on the way West,
standing as high as a horse's knees,
waving flags of peace and serenity
in a world gone angry and red.

To Mark Rothko from the Chapel

I enter your octagon again this morning.
Sit on a bench. Float among the planes.
Meditate in this holy space without religion,
without crosses, only fourteen black paintings
in this small, silent, windowless place.
Time hangs by gossamer threads of thought.

You designed it so nothing distracts the mind,
no artificial boundaries, no bright museum glare,
only a muted glow from the skylight and floating
rectangles of deep purple and black—perfect absorbers of light,
color of night, ancient caves, charcoal, burnt bones,
sealed tombs, underworld, holes in the universe.

Everything here invites contemplation—of life, death,
eternity, whether there is an eternity. I feel sorrow
in the black spaces. I feel comfort in their existence.
You created all of this for us, then left it, left us,
left the obelisk purposely unfinished, broken.
You spoke of truth, freedom, justice. Such anarchy.

Vandals saw only darkness in your work, splashed
white paint by the entrance, left handbills that read
"It's okay to be white." They did not understand that
white is the sum of all colors of light. I pray for them
and the world in this sanctuary of sacred beauty.
In the stillness you created, I rise to meet you.

Color Me Red

In this gray world, I need more red:
A Northern Cardinal perched on a tree branch
Red roses in spring
Ripe tomatoes in summertime
Sumac leaves in autumn
Berries on a Pyracantha bush in winter
The crimson scarf a friend gave to me
A valentine from a long-ago lover
Lipstick I wear with a black dress
A suitcase to stand out from the rest
The setting sun with desert dust
The steep metal roof rising in a green valley
The apple I pluck from a tree and bite into sweet flesh
The blood of my ancestors pulsing through me
Their blood soaked into the soil of history
Seeping out of me from the rose's thorn
Red, so red

The Edge of Ambedo

All day worldly terrors gnaw at me.
The blinking screen screams war, pandemic,
murder, madness. Lost souls swirl
in a murmuration of chaos.

I flee outside into the wild peace.
A Monarch flutters from flower to flower,
probing purple mistflower for nectar.
Fly, alight, sip; fly, alight, sip.

Delicate wings bear me to the edge of ambedo.
I step off and float like a butterfly over the abyss.
The Monarch shows me how to find sustenance.
Fly, alight, suck life's sweetness before it vanishes.

Nature Is a Serial Killer

Autumn, when the purple mistflower and orange cosmos
take over the garden, standing a foot or more tall,
sweet sustenance for the annual migration.

The nectar calls first the Queens, then the Monarchs.
I walk among the flowers and the butterflies flutter
around me until I feel like I'm in a dream.

I put the Monarchs in my viewfinder, zooming in
on their wings with patterns like stained glass
attached to black-and-white spotted bodies.

Their long proboscis probes the flowers. I focus on
a large Monarch as it begins moving down the stem
of a cosmos. I frame the shot, release the shutter.

Then I see it, a green praying mantis hidden in the leaves,
holding the Monarch with its barbed forelegs,
pulling off the wings and nibbling the soft flesh.

The Monarchs return to the fringed flowers all autumn,
oblivious to what lies below. I hold my camera, waiting
for the moment of capture as the mantises wait for theirs.

Wild Solace

This world of doors, of rooms with no views,
of lights in the ceiling instead of sun and sky
leaves me choking on dust, gasping for air.

When darkness falls I fling off my clothes,
becoming naked like an animal,
unlocking the door, plunging into the blue moonlight.

Coyotes howl, owls hoot, night creatures
join the chirping, screeching chorus,
beckoning me to join them in the wild solace.

Soft grass caresses bare feet, lushness envelops me.
I breathe in the pure night smells of earth cooling,
of distant rain carried on the wind.

I feel unseen hearts beating, eyes staring in the dark.
Let me lie here, let me die here in the wild tangle
instead of a room with no windows, gasping for air.

Elegy for a Once-Wild Place

The inevitable is coming;
we unknowingly brought it with us.
Did we really think we could flee
to this wild place and no one would follow?
We cannot close the gates now.

Bulldozers uproot cedar on hillsides,
chainsaws buzz, trucks rumble
over cattle guards. Old ranch houses
crumble, while skeletons of new homes
sprout from limestone hills.

The little goatherd and windmill
down the road disappeared, replaced
by Black Angus, a metal shed full of hay,
protected by a locked gate and a
"No Trespassing" sign.

They come with satellite dishes,
Internet towers, King Ranch-edition trucks.
More white-tailed deer lie by the highway,
graceful necks broken. One died
by our mailbox and bloated in the sun.

High game fences inch toward us,
tall power poles creep up the highway,
paved roads slice up the landscape.
We are all refugees now, fleeing like deer,
searching for a piece of the last wild place.

Continuum

I am sunrise
       throwing across hills
       spinning blue whirl again
       waking birds in trees
I am sunset
       lassoing fire in blue sky
       pushing it to the horizon
       sinking sun in a coral sea
I am twilight
       unfurling violet
       sprinkling night ice
       howling with coyotes
I am lake
       glimmering, deep and clear
       anticipating the dive
       reflecting cloudscape
I am river
       flowing from springs
       longing for paddle strokes
       meandering to sea
I am spring
       hatching
       summer buzzing
       autumn goldening
       winter silvering
I am love
       you never lost it
       it was here
       around you
       all this time

About the Author

Kathryn Jones' poetry has appeared in numerous print and online literary journals, including TexasPoetryAssignment.org, *Unbroken*, and the *Langdon Review of the Arts in Texas*; anthologies *Unknotting the Line: The Poetry in Prose* (Dos Gatos Press, 2023); *Odes and Elegies: Eco-Poetry from the Texas Gulf Coast* (Lamar University Press, 2021); and *Lone Star Poetry* (Kallisto Gaia Press, 2022); and a chapbook, *An Orchid's Guide to Life* (Finishing Line Press, 2024).

A longtime journalist, Jones also has written for *The New York Times, Texas Monthly* magazine, *The Dallas Morning News*, and many other publications. Her essays have been published in books about film, literature, and songwriting.

She was inducted into the Texas Institute of Letters in 2016 and lives on a ranch in Bosque County, Texas.

Kathryn Jones's most recent collection of verse, The Solace of Wild Places, reinforces her identity as a poet-naturalist. Jones finds longing and sanctuary in the flora and fauna described in her poems. In "Shell Hunting," for instance, she can hear her "mother's voice floating on the sea," and in "The Art of Stillness" she immerses herself in "the sweetness of doing nothing." Jones explores other places, too, such as the state of sleeplessness in "Insomnia." These powerful and intimate intrigues with physical and emotional spaces continue to resonate strongly beyond the initial reading.

—Betsy Joseph, author of Relatively Speaking

With Kathryn Jones as my guide, I have been a fortunate traveler in these poems, following her across Texas from its shores to its canyons, from its deserts to its hilltops, my attention drawn by her to the smallest detail of feathery seeds and to the immense turquoise skies of our state. Certainly, we made a few detours along the way out west to the highlands of New Mexico with their special beauty and grace, but it's Texas I think where the wild places sing to her, comforting and true.

—Laurence Musgrove, author of A Stranger's Heart and editor of The Senior
Class: 100 Poets on Aging

With painstaking clarity, Kathryn Jones brings us specialties from the natural world, particularly those of the Southwest. Jones celebrates personal encounters, identifying in precise detail animals and plants. pathways and terrains. Holding a fossil in hand, hearing nearby "creatures chirping, howling, singing like a choir," she turns the universal into the personal, with a tapestry of inviting colors, textures, situations, and feelings. Read these poems to be reminded of the ageless wild free places deserving commemoration in our time.

—Jan Seale, 2012 Texas Poet Laureate

In this vivid collection of poems, Kathryn Jones testifies to the wondrous nature of the world she experiences, from the migrating birds and intricate shells on the Texas Gulf Coast to the stark beauties of the desert and mountains of New Mexico. While camping out at Big Bend with friends, she notes that "We, such tiny figures in a boundless landscape, / felt our human insignificance and reveled in it." Her poems are themselves full of thoughtful revelations.

—Chip Dameron, author of Waiting for an Etcher